WOULD YOU RATHER...?

Contents

1.

Incredibly Icky Would You Rather

Would you rather...

poop in your hand
OR
poop in someone else's hands?

Would you rather...

sniff a dog's butt
OR
lick a dog's butt?

Would you rather...

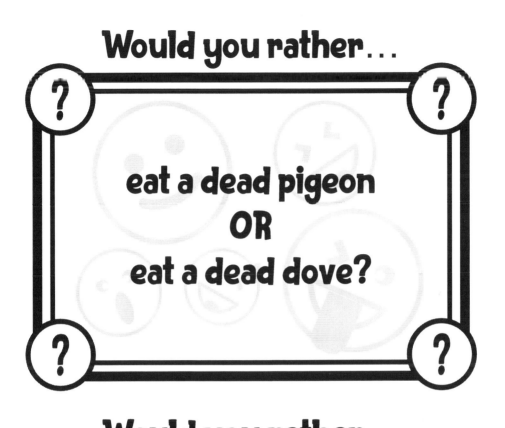

eat a dead pigeon
OR
eat a dead dove?

Would you rather...

have a dozen
cockroaches run over
your hands
OR
run over your legs?

Would you rather...

give a bath to a dead body
OR
sleep all night beside a dead body?

Would you rather...

lick a handful of sand
OR
eat a handful of sand?

Would you rather...

get married to a zombie
OR
have a zombie baby?

Would you rather...

have blood come out of
the shower
OR
take a bath full of blood?

Would you rather...

bleed from your eyes
OR
bleed from your toenails?

Would you rather...

run from a poisonous snake
OR
carry a poisonous snake around your neck?

Would you rather...

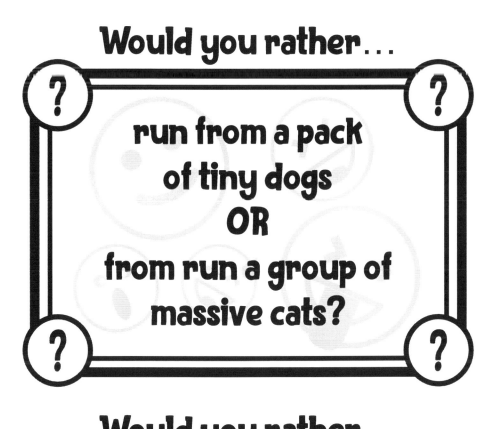

run from a pack
of tiny dogs
OR
from run a group of
massive cats?

Would you rather...

drink a glass of sweat
OR
eat a chunk of hair?

Would you rather...

keep a deceased family member's head on a shelf

OR

keep their pickled heart in a jar?

Would you rather...

have a long tail

OR

have two horns on your forehead?

Would you rather…

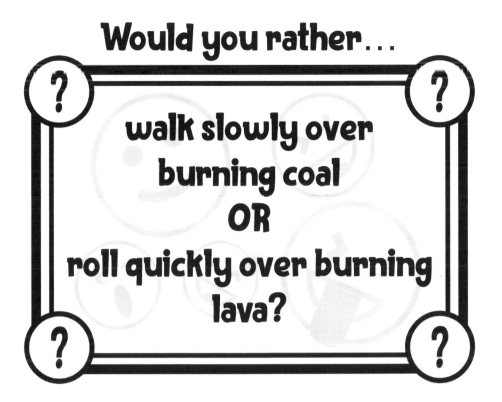

**walk slowly over
burning coal
OR
roll quickly over burning
lava?**

Would you rather…

**find a decomposed body
in your refrigerator
OR
a freshly dead body in
your closet?**

Would you rather...

wake up in a dark and smelly box
OR
wake up a bathroom with a blocked toilet?

Would you rather...

be stuck in a cage stuffed with cockroaches
OR
stuck in a cage piled with ants?

Would you rather...

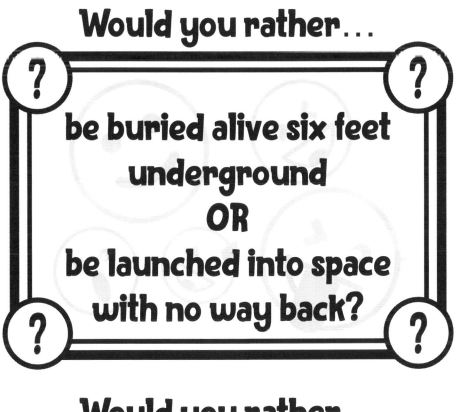

be buried alive six feet
underground
OR
be launched into space
with no way back?

Would you rather...

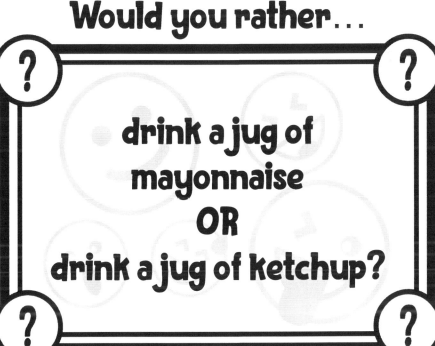

drink a jug of
mayonnaise
OR
drink a jug of ketchup?

Would you rather...

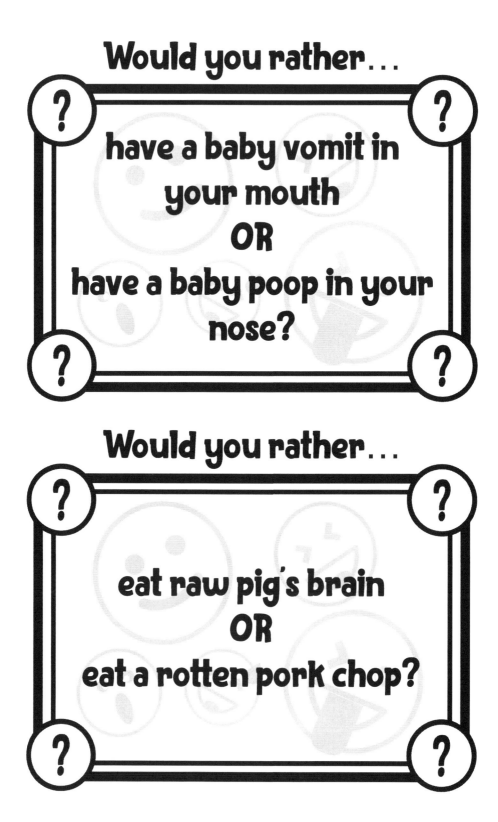

have a baby vomit in your mouth
OR
have a baby poop in your nose?

Would you rather...

eat raw pig's brain
OR
eat a rotten pork chop?

Would you rather...

have a piranha
bite your toe
OR
have a piranha bite your
finger?

Would you rather...

chew someone else's
toenail
OR
suck on someone else's
toe?

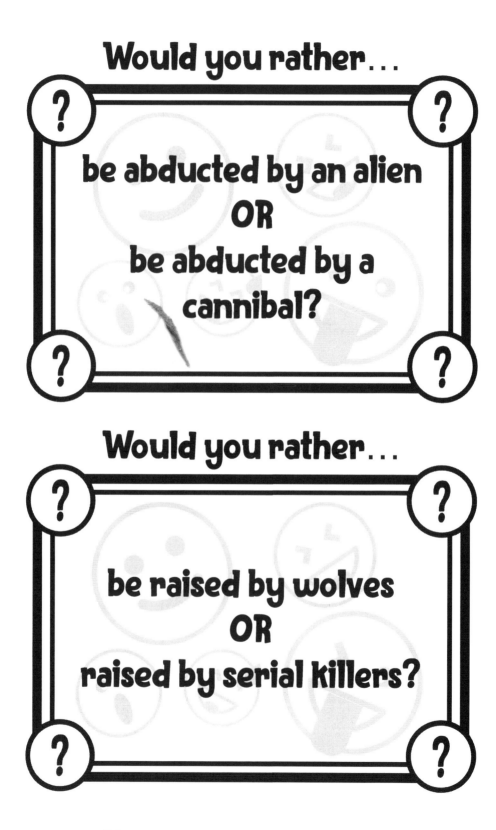

Would you rather...

be abducted by an alien
OR
be abducted by a cannibal?

Would you rather...

be raised by wolves
OR
raised by serial killers?

Would you rather...

drink dirty water every day OR eat dirty food every day?

Would you rather...

eat somebody else's boogers OR eat somebody else's toenail clippings?

Would you rather...

poop in your pants
OR
poop in a portable toilet
full to the top?

Would you rather...

have constantly itchy
armpits
OR
have constantly smelly
armpits?

Would you rather...

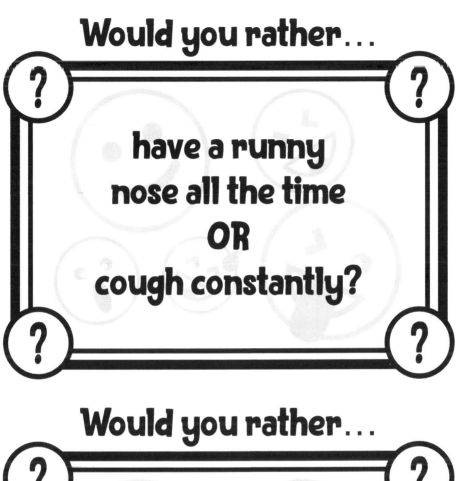

have a runny
nose all the time
OR
cough constantly?

Would you rather...

lick a goat's beard
OR
lick a goat's tail?

Would you rather...

have a massive pimple on your nose
OR
have a massive pimple on your butt?

Would you rather...

use a public toilet when you have diarrhea
OR
have a stranger with diarrhea use your toilet?

Would you rather...

**have sweaty feet
OR
have sweaty hands?**

Would you rather...

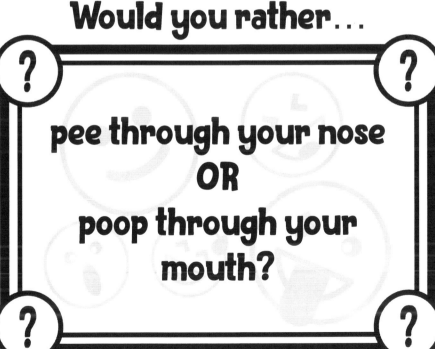

**pee through your nose
OR
poop through your
mouth?**

Would you rather...

find blood in your poo
OR
find blood in your pee?

Would you rather...

have someone sneeze in
your face
OR
fart in your face?

Would you rather...

swallow a whole worm
OR stick your tongue in a
jar of warms?

Would you rather...

pee when you laugh
OR
laugh when you pee?

Would you rather...

not shower for a month
OR
not poo for a week?

Would you rather...

lick a toilet seat
OR
lick a toilet floor?

2.

Ridiculously Rotten Would You Rather

Would you rather...

swim in a pool filled with
garbage
or take a shower in
spoiled milk?

Would you rather...

drink a spider smoothie
OR
eat a roaster cockroach?

Would you rather...

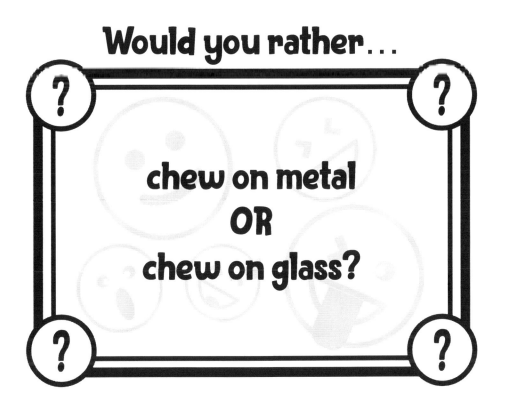

chew on metal
OR
chew on glass?

Would you rather...

smell dirty baby diapers
OR
smell dirty adult
diapers?

Would you rather...

cut a lump out of your
skin with a knife
OR
poke it out with a
needle?

Would you rather...

find hair in the
food you are eating
OR
find a cockroach in your
food?

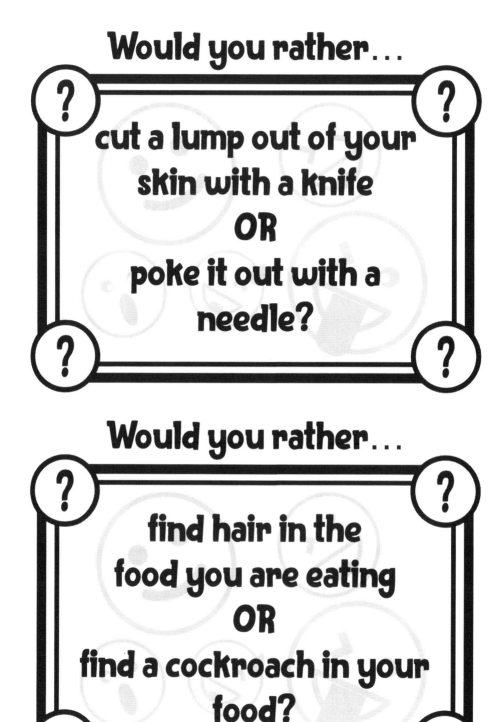

Would you rather...

lick a frozen pee pop
OR
sip hot pee tea?

Would you rather...

roll around on
crushed glass
OR
roll around in burned
dog poo?

Would you rather...

eat chocolate flavored poo
OR
eat poo flavored chocolate?

Would you rather...

rub a chili pepper in your eye
OR
suck on a chili pepper all day?

Would you rather...

have somebody bite
your nose off
OR
have somebody bit your
ear off?

Would you rather...

pee in a bottle
OR
pee in a can?

Would you rather...

have an oozy rash on
your face
OR
have an oozy rash on
your bottom?

Would you rather...

drop your phone in a
dirty toilet
OR
drop your phone in dog
poo?

Would you rather...

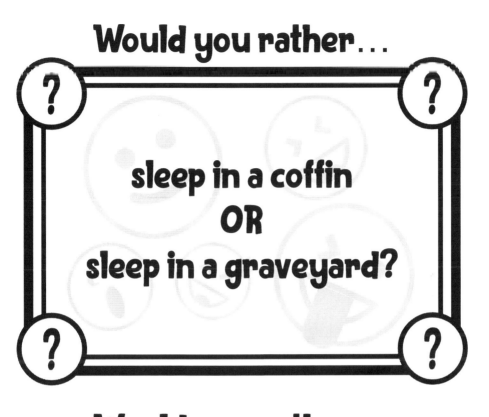

sleep in a coffin
OR
sleep in a graveyard?

Would you rather...

never wash your hair
for the rest of your life
OR
wash your hair with
toothpaste?

Would you rather...

be the ugliest person
in the world
OR
the smelliest person in
the world?

Would you rather...

have your forehead
pierced
OR
have your bottom
pierced?

Would you rather...

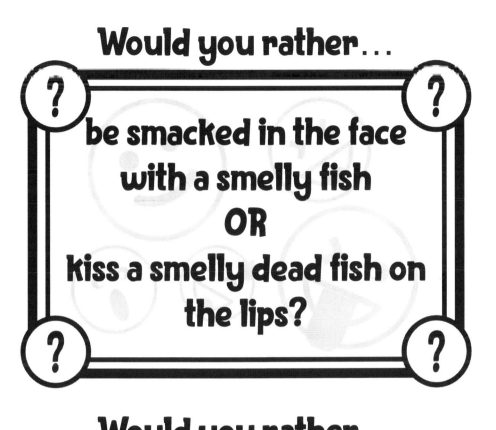

be smacked in the face
with a smelly fish
OR
kiss a smelly dead fish on
the lips?

Would you rather...

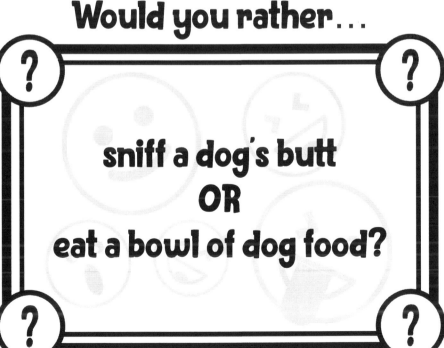

sniff a dog's butt
OR
eat a bowl of dog food?

Would you rather...

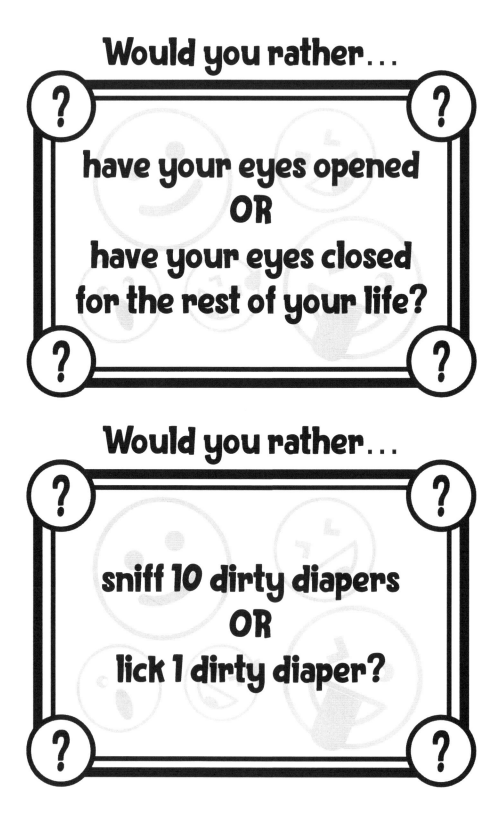

have your eyes opened
OR
have your eyes closed
for the rest of your life?

Would you rather...

sniff 10 dirty diapers
OR
lick 1 dirty diaper?

Would you rather...

always be constipated
OR
always be farting?

Would you rather...

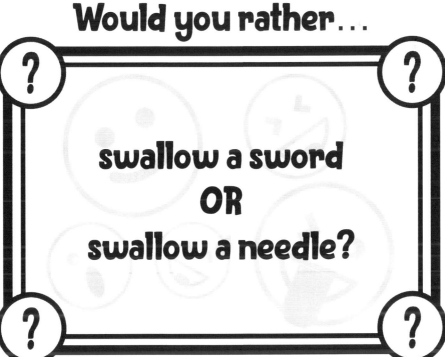

swallow a sword
OR
swallow a needle?

Would you rather...

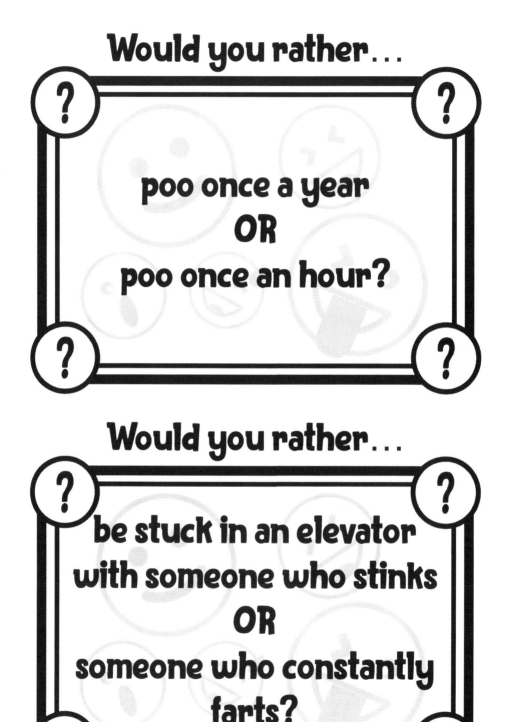

poo once a year
OR
poo once an hour?

Would you rather...

be stuck in an elevator
with someone who stinks
OR
someone who constantly
farts?

Would you rather...

drink a liter of pee
OR
drink a liter of sweat?

Would you rather...

have an elephant trunk
OR
a giraffe neck?

Would you rather...

eat poison ivy
OR
eat a handful of wasps?

Would you rather...

have a hairy face
OR
have hair all over the
rest of your body?

Would you rather...

**die by zombie attack
OR
die by shark attack?**

Would you rather...

**speak in grunts
OR
pound your chest?**

Would you rather...

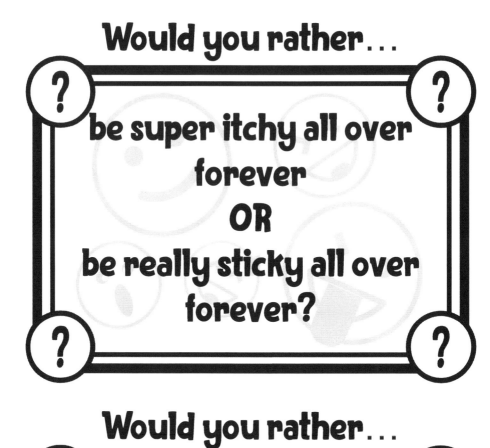

be super itchy all over forever

OR

be really sticky all over forever?

Would you rather...

have your farts
be super loud
and smell like nothing

OR

be silent and smell
terrible?

Would you rather...

eat an entire bag of
rotting flies
OR
have live flies come out
every time you sneezed?

Would you rather...

peel off all the scabs a
hobo has
OR
suck on socks that are
full of feet sweat?

Would you rather...

be inside a porta-potty
when it falls over
OR
step in dog poop with
bare feet?

Would you rather...

eat a hamburger from
the trash
OR
drink a can of soda from
the trash?

Would you rather…

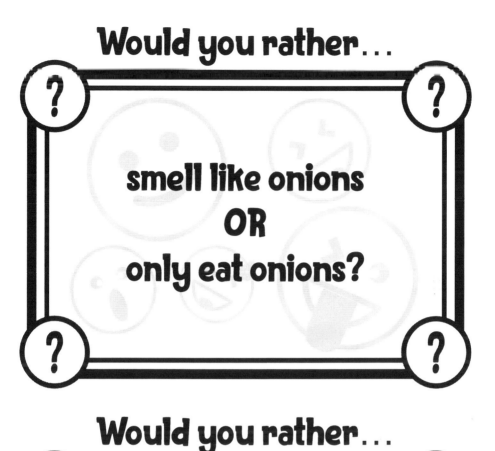

**smell like onions
OR
only eat onions?**

Would you rather…

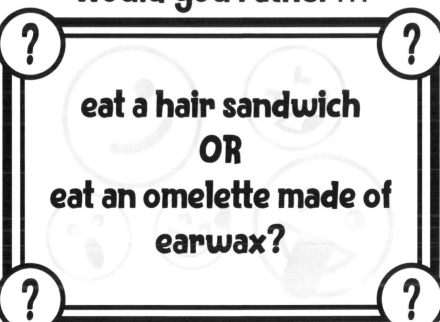

**eat a hair sandwich
OR
eat an omelette made of
earwax?**

Would you rather...

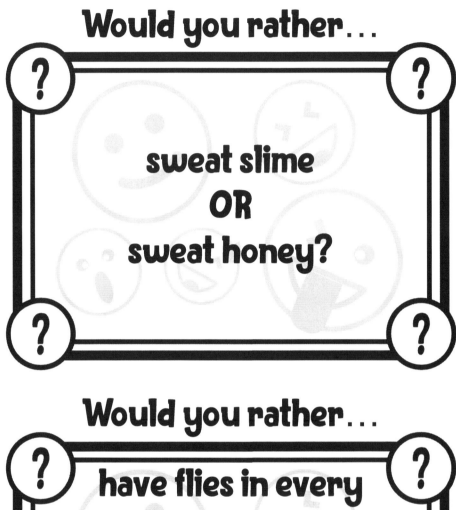

sweat slime
OR
sweat honey?

Would you rather...

have flies in every
ice cube of your drink
OR
use an unwashed tuna
fish can for all your
drinks?

3.

Disastrously Disgusting Would You Rather

Would you rather...

stick your hands in a
bowl of eyeballs
OR
a bowl of brains?

Would you rather...

drink a glass of
super-spicy mustard
OR
eat a hamburger you
found in a public
bathroom?

Would you rather...

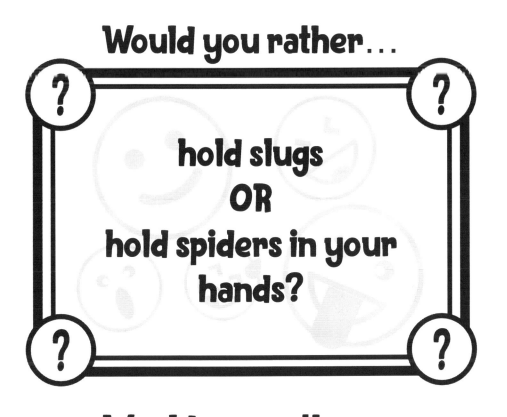

hold slugs
OR
hold spiders in your hands?

Would you rather...

have greasy hair that constantly drips oil
OR
have a non-stop drooling problem?

Would you rather...

rub vinegar
OR
rub hot sauce all over
your body?

Would you rather...

eat a live snake
OR
eat a dead jellyfish?

Would you rather...

**sleep in a pig sty
OR
sleep next to a skunk?**

Would you rather...

**suck the drool off the face of
a dog just back from a run
OR
share a bowl of dog food with
a dog eating at the same
time?**

Would you rather...

ride a farting horse
OR
walk a vomiting dog?

Would you rather...

always have thick white
coating on your tongue
OR
have a slimy film
covering your eyes?

Would you rather…

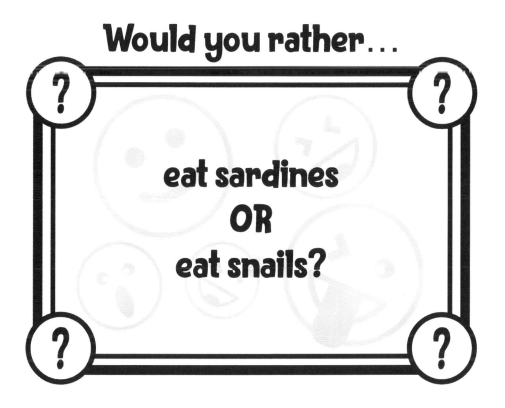

eat sardines
OR
eat snails?

Would you rather…

spread your nose
pickings on your cereal
OR
put pieces of your
earwax on your pizza?

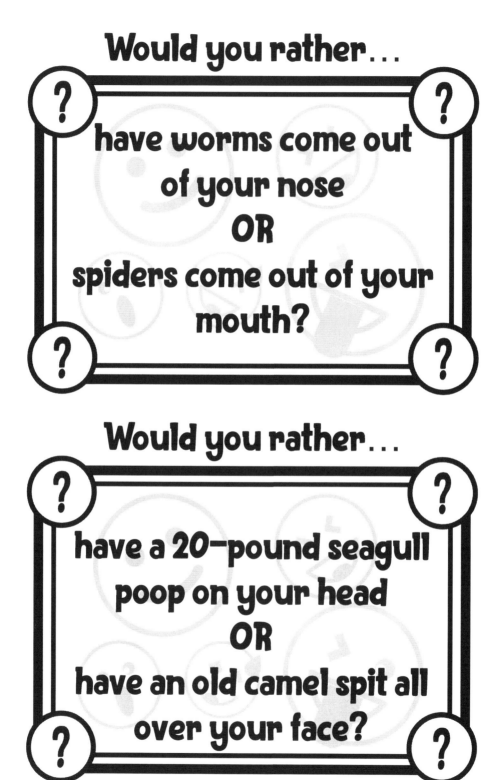

Would you rather...

have worms come out
of your nose
OR
spiders come out of your
mouth?

Would you rather...

have a 20-pound seagull
poop on your head
OR
have an old camel spit all
over your face?

Would you rather...

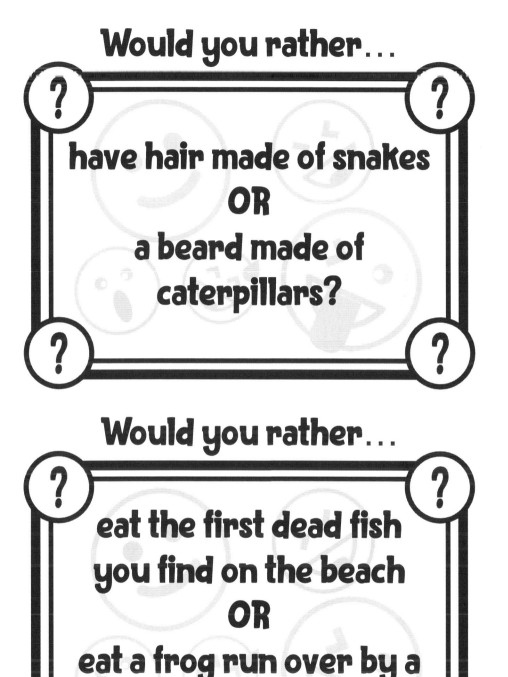

have hair made of snakes
OR
a beard made of caterpillars?

Would you rather...

eat the first dead fish you find on the beach
OR
eat a frog run over by a car?

Would you rather...

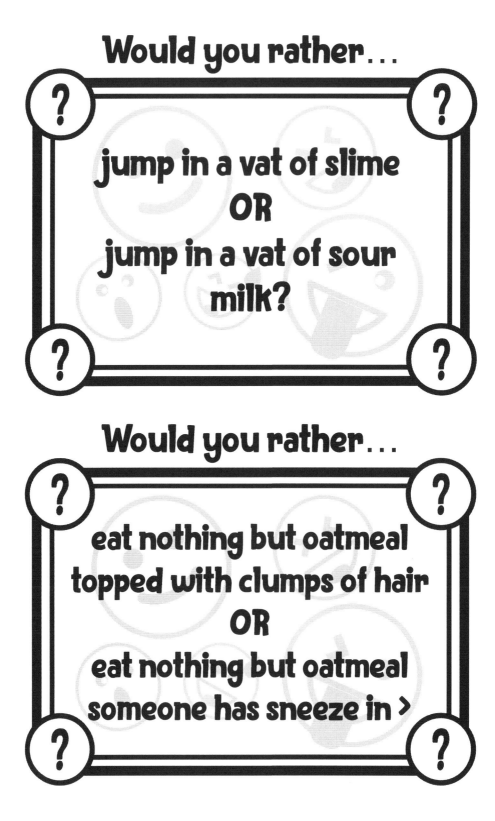

jump in a vat of slime
OR
jump in a vat of sour milk?

Would you rather...

eat nothing but oatmeal topped with clumps of hair
OR
eat nothing but oatmeal someone has sneeze in >

Would you rather...

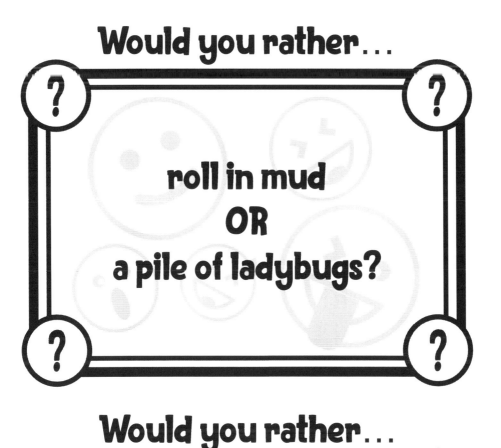

roll in mud
OR
a pile of ladybugs?

Would you rather...

have dry crust around
your eyes
OR
oozing crust around
your nose?

Would you rather...

feel itchy behind your
ears
OR
feel itchy on your feet?

Would you rather...

drink liquid leaking from a
trash bag
OR
chew on a strange wet
clump found in the sofa?

Would you rather...

use sandpaper for toilet paper
OR
use sticky tape?

Would you rather...

eat 10 pounds of cheese
OR
eat a bucket of peanut?

Would you rather...

drink water from a vase
with dead flowers
OR
eat the flowers?

Would you rather...

eat fried monkey brains
OR
eat the raw guts from a
huge snake?

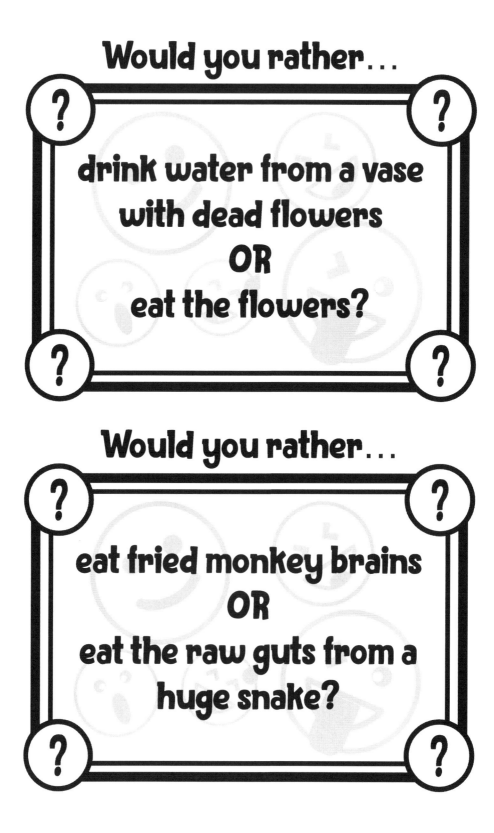

Would you rather...

**always wear wet socks
OR
always wear wet underwear?**

Would you rather...

**drink 8 cups of old dirty aquarium water
OR
squeeze the dirty water from a sponge into your mouth**

Would you rather...

drink milk from a cow's
udder
OR
drink milk that has gone
off?

Would you rather...

chew a piece of toenail
off a man's dirty foot
OR
lick every inch of his
unwashed hair back?

Would you rather...

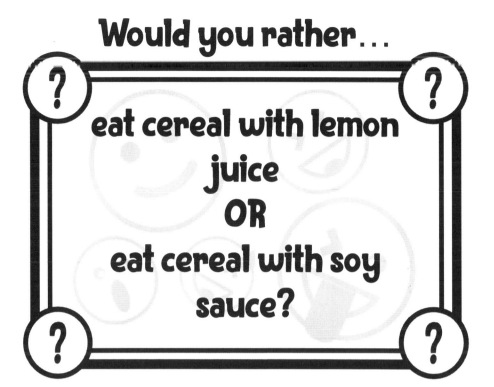

eat cereal with lemon juice
OR
eat cereal with soy sauce?

Would you rather...

always have cold sores on your lips
OR
always have oozing sores on your hands?

Would you rather…

have lice in your hair
OR
rats living in your walls?

Would you rather…

have someone sneeze
directly into your mouth
OR
have somebody clean your
ear with their tongue?

Would you rather...

have blue-colored pee
OR
green colored poop?

Would you rather...

drink a cup of pus from
a huge blister
OR
eat a salad topped with
"Bits O' Scabs?"

Would you rather…

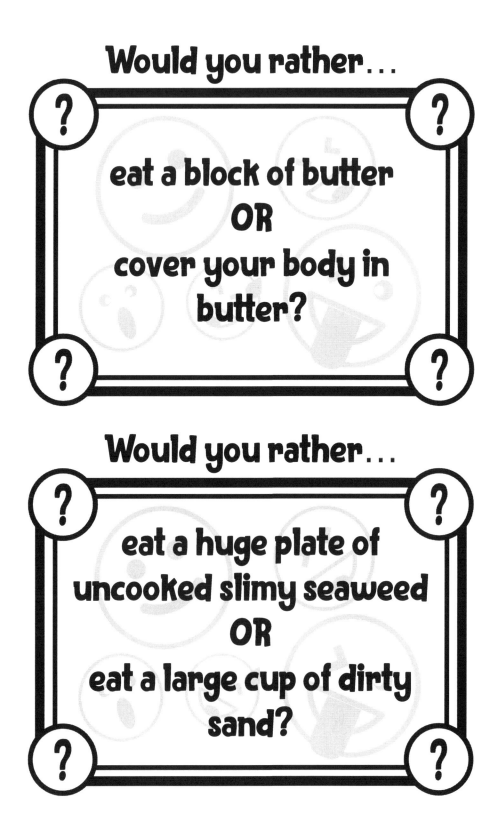

eat a block of butter
OR
cover your body in butter?

Would you rather…

eat a huge plate of uncooked slimy seaweed
OR
eat a large cup of dirty sand?

Would you rather...

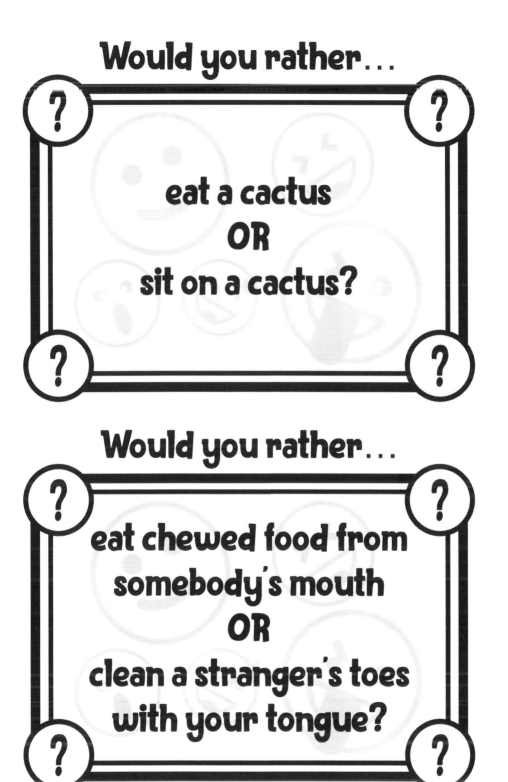

eat a cactus
OR
sit on a cactus?

Would you rather...

eat chewed food from
somebody's mouth
OR
clean a stranger's toes
with your tongue?

Would you rather...

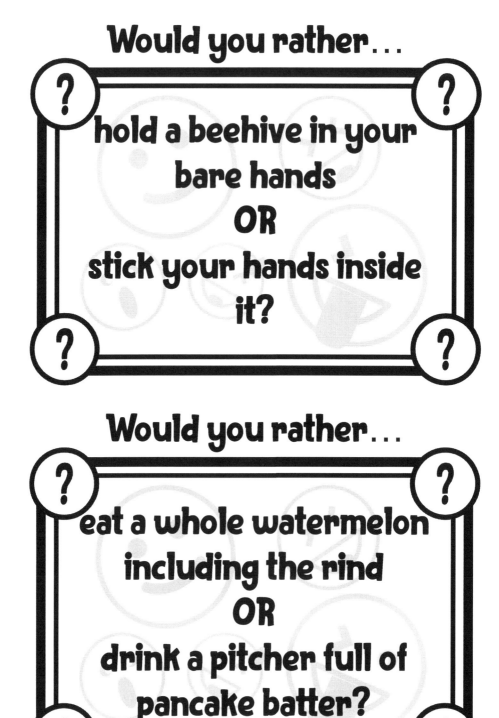

hold a beehive in your bare hands
OR
stick your hands inside it?

Would you rather...

eat a whole watermelon including the rind
OR
drink a pitcher full of pancake batter?

Would you rather...

eat your friend's nose hairs

OR

eat your friend's nail clippings?

Would you rather...

clean your refrigerator with your tongue

OR

lick the makeup off of a clown's face?

Would you rather...

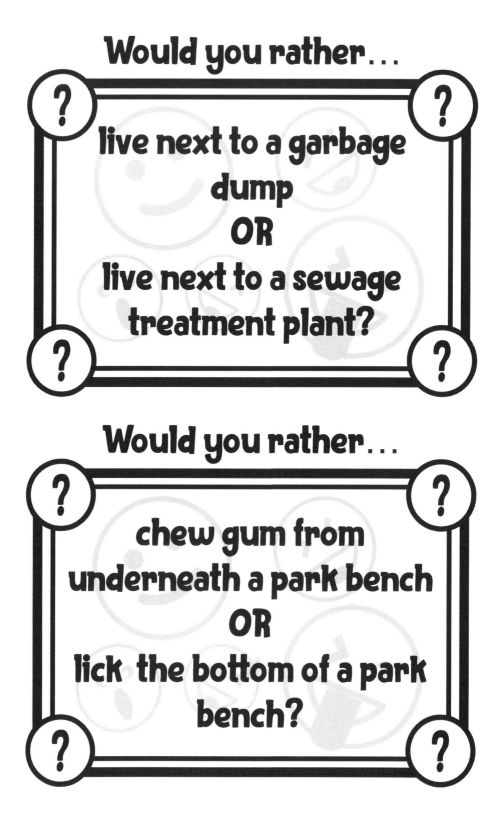

live next to a garbage
dump
OR
live next to a sewage
treatment plant?

Would you rather...

chew gum from
underneath a park bench
OR
lick the bottom of a park
bench?

Would you rather...

eat food off the ground
in the rain
OR
use your dirty feet to eat
food off a table?

Would you rather...

eat piping hot pizza
OR
eat a pizza that is burned
black?

Would you rather...

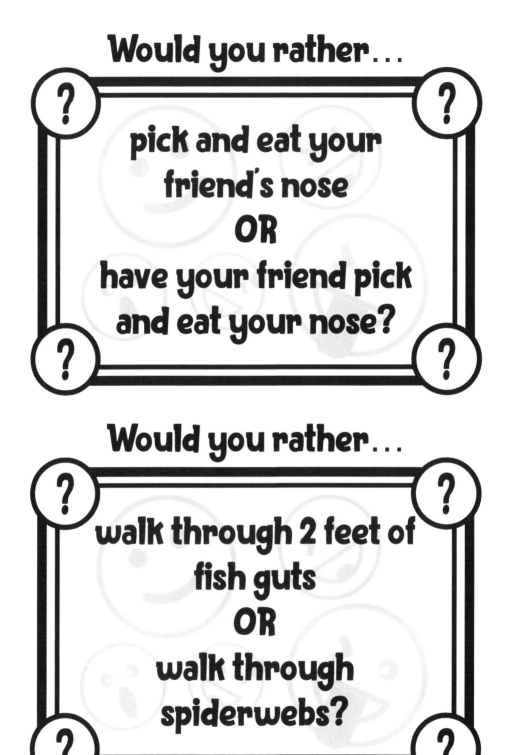

pick and eat your
friend's nose
OR
have your friend pick
and eat your nose?

Would you rather...

walk through 2 feet of
fish guts
OR
walk through
spiderwebs?

Would you rather...

freeze to death
OR
burn to death?

Would you rather...

have finger fungus
OR
have warts on your
nose?

Would you rather...

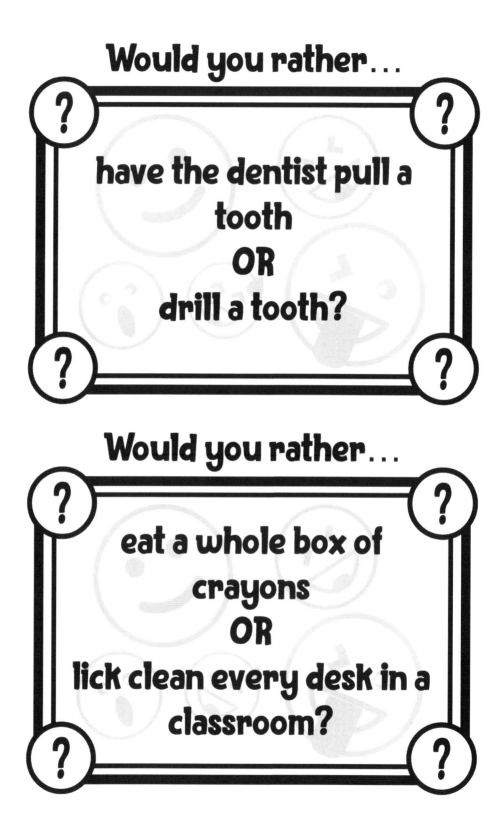

have the dentist pull a tooth
OR
drill a tooth?

Would you rather...

eat a whole box of crayons
OR
lick clean every desk in a classroom?

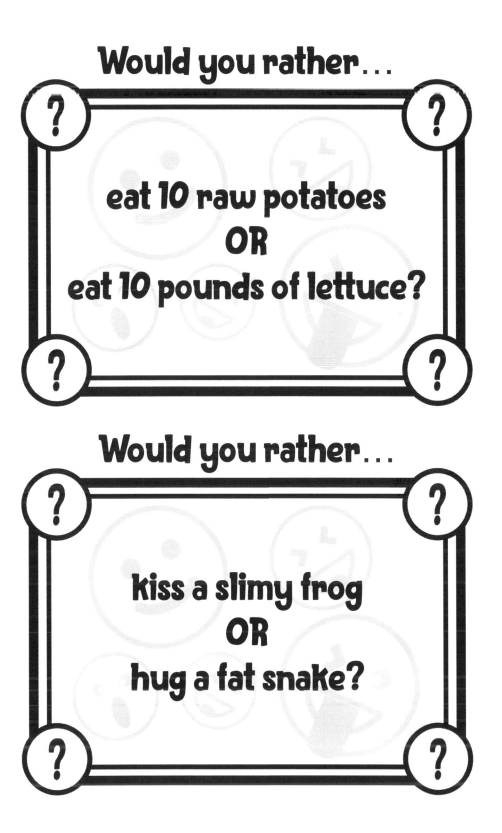

Would you rather…

eat 10 raw potatoes
OR
eat 10 pounds of lettuce?

Would you rather…

kiss a slimy frog
OR
hug a fat snake?

Would you rather...

have teeth as big as computer keys

OR

have eyeballs the size of tennis balls?

Would you rather...

be buried in snow

OR

buried in sand?

Would you rather...

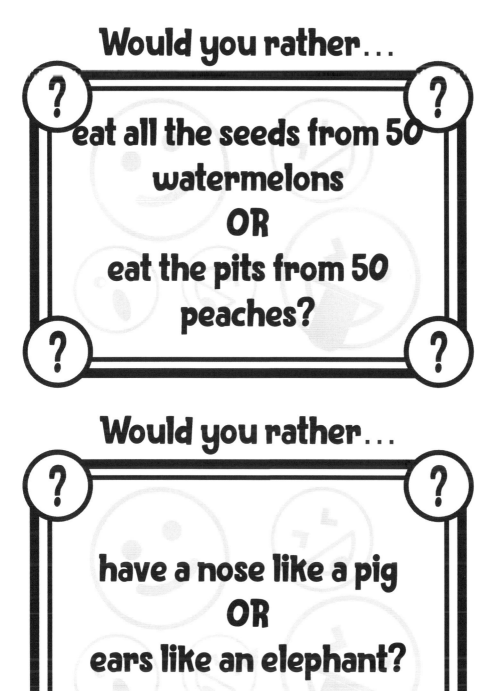

eat all the seeds from 50 watermelons
OR
eat the pits from 50 peaches?

Would you rather...

have a nose like a pig
OR
ears like an elephant?

Would you rather...

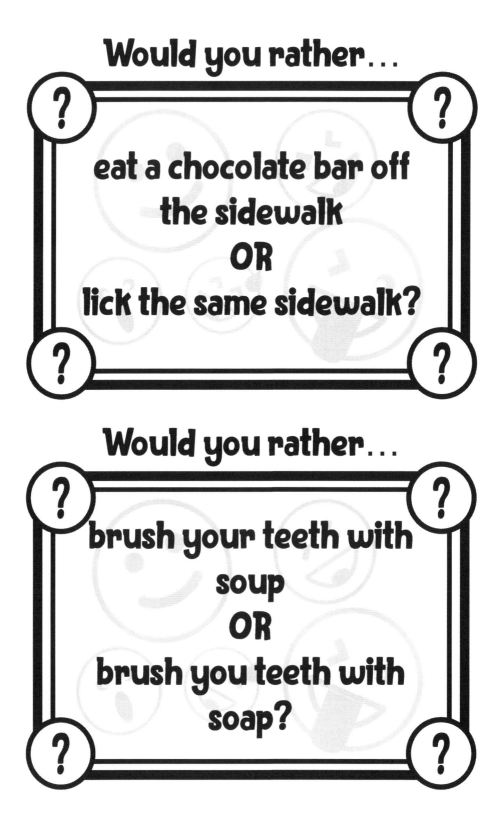

eat a chocolate bar off
the sidewalk
OR
lick the same sidewalk?

Would you rather...

brush your teeth with
soup
OR
brush you teeth with
soap?

Would you rather...

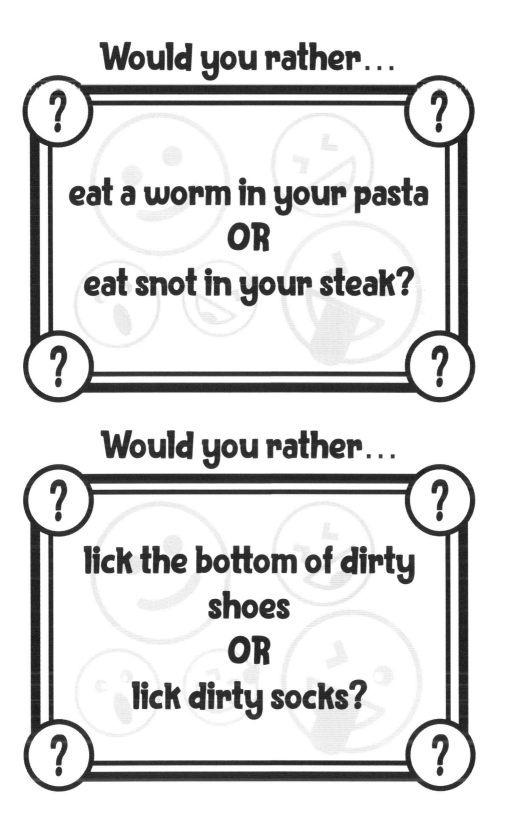

eat a worm in your pasta
OR
eat snot in your steak?

Would you rather...

lick the bottom of dirty
shoes
OR
lick dirty socks?

Would you rather...

burp every time you see
somebody
OR
fart every 5 minutes?

Would you rather...

have bright yellow teeth
OR
have bright yellow
eyes?

Would you rather...

never take a shower
OR
never brush your teeth?

Would you rather...

eat 20 banana peels
OR
eat 20 orange peels?

Would you rather...

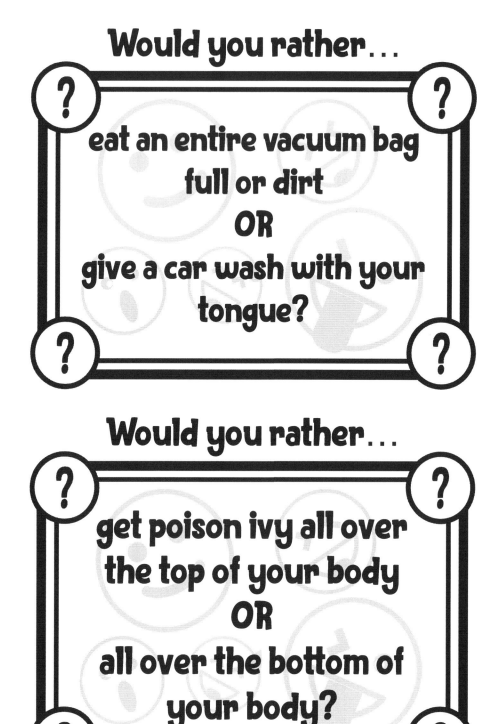

eat an entire vacuum bag full or dirt
OR
give a car wash with your tongue?

Would you rather...

get poison ivy all over the top of your body
OR
all over the bottom of your body?

Would you rather...

eat the drool of a baby
while he eats boiled cabbage
OR
drink pea soup dripping
from an old man's beard?

Would you rather...

have a bee sting on your
nose
OR
10 mosquito bites on your
ear?

Would you rather...

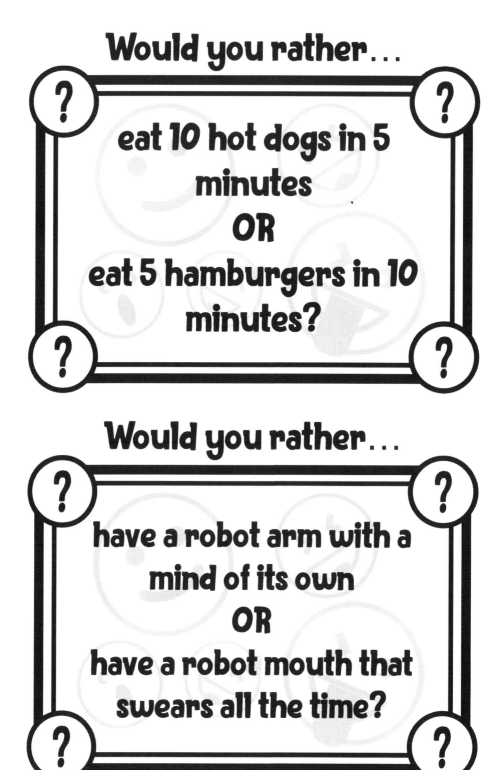

eat **10** hot dogs in **5** minutes

OR

eat **5** hamburgers in **10** minutes?

Would you rather...

have a robot arm with a mind of its own

OR

have a robot mouth that swears all the time?

Would you rather...

find half a worm in an
apple you're eating
OR
eat half a banana full of
fly eggs?

Would you rather...

drink a cup of seawater
OR
drink a pitcher of toilet
water?

Would you rather...

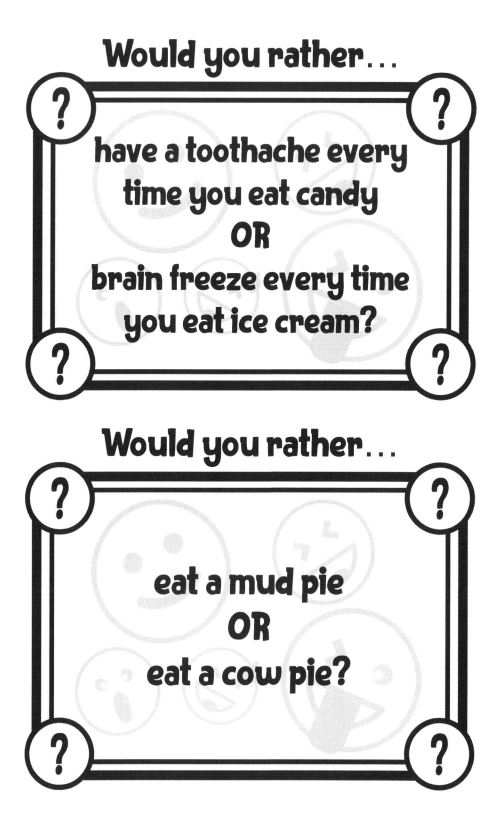

have a toothache every
time you eat candy
OR
brain freeze every time
you eat ice cream?

Would you rather...

eat a mud pie
OR
eat a cow pie?

Would you rather...

pee in your pants at the
shopping mall
OR
poop in your pants at a
bus stop?

Would you rather...

drink a glass of sour milk
OR
eat a head of rotten
lettuce?

4.

Amazingly Awful Would You Rather

Would you rather...

clean golf balls in your
mouth
OR
clean silverware in your
mouth?

Would you rather...

leave a trail of slime
everywhere you go
OR
leave a trail of rabbit poop
everywhere you go?

Would you rather...

use vinegar to wash
your hair
OR
use cat pee to wash your
hands?

Would you rather...

find a cockroach in your
shirt?
OR
find a mouse crawling
inside your pants?

Would you rather...

chew gum in your mouth
every time you eat
OR
take a sip of soy sauce with
every drink?

Would you rather...

put on a hat full of raw
egg yolks
OR
pull on a pair of shoes
filled with egg whites?

Would you rather...

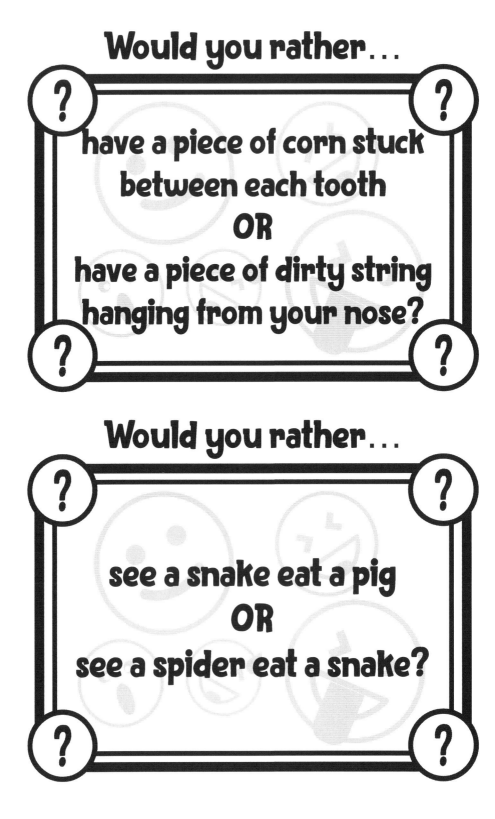

have a piece of corn stuck between each tooth
OR
have a piece of dirty string hanging from your nose?

Would you rather...

see a snake eat a pig
OR
see a spider eat a snake?

Would you rather...

wear diapers on your head and **NOT** use them
OR
wear diapers on your bottom and use them?

Would you rather...

have 12 fingers
OR
have 8 toes?

Would you rather...

always feel like you have to sneeze
OR
always feel like you have the hiccups?

Would you rather...

jump in a bathtub of full of ice water
OR
warm baby pee?

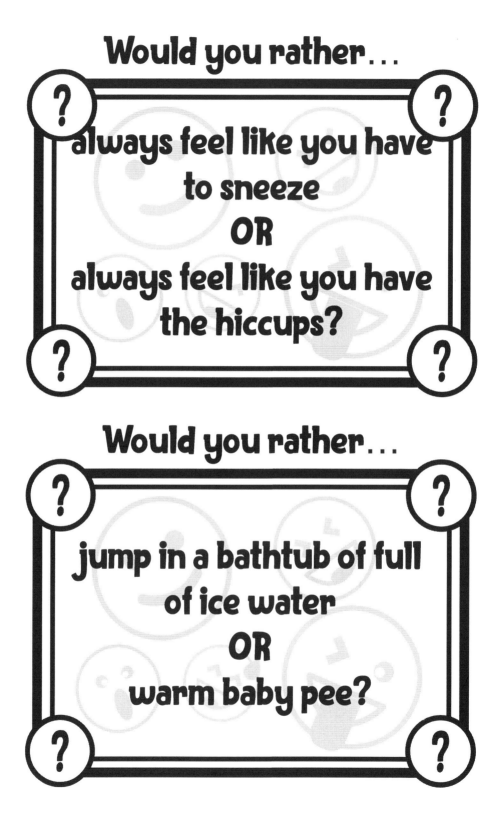

Would you rather...

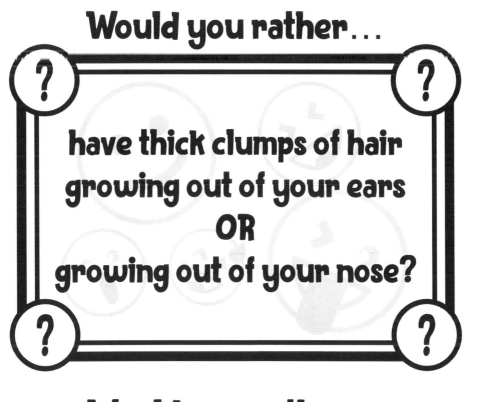

have thick clumps of hair
growing out of your ears
OR
growing out of your nose?

Would you rather...

sleep upside down next
to a bat
OR
sleep lying down next to
a rat?

Would you rather...

drink a cup of maple
syrup
OR
drink a cup of honey?

Would you rather...

find a beehive in your
hair
OR
a lizard living in your
ear?

Would you rather...

chop onions every
morning for an hour
OR
eat raw onions every
day for breakfast?

Would you rather...

have it rain caterpillars
OR
have chickens fall from
the sky?

Would you rather...

eat one piece of rotten
fruit
OR
eat 4 slices of rotten
bread?

Would you rather...

wake up covered in
slimy snails
OR
fall asleep with ants
crawling on you?

Would you rather…

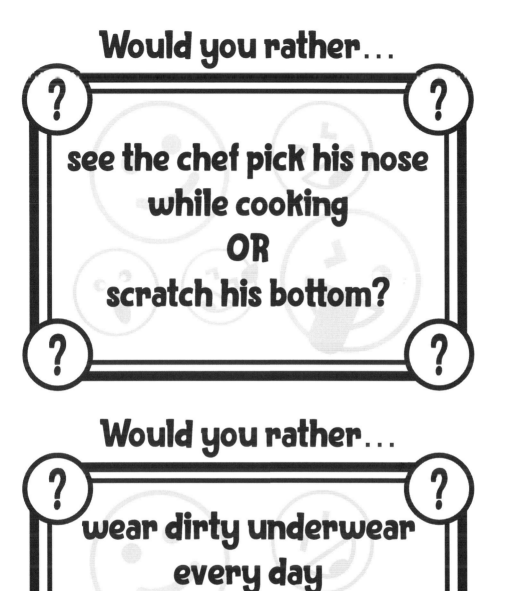

see the chef pick his nose
while cooking
OR
scratch his bottom?

Would you rather…

wear dirty underwear
every day
OR
wear stinky socks every
day?

Would you rather…

be covered in lizard skin
OR
be covered in cat fur?

Would you rather…

lick a firefighter's dirty
underwear
OR
drink sweat from a
firefighter's dirty boots?

Would you rather...

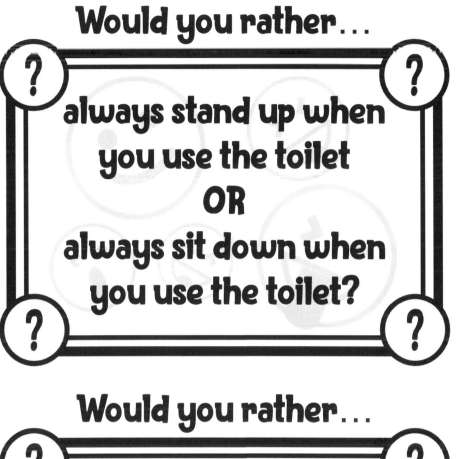

always stand up when
you use the toilet
OR
always sit down when
you use the toilet?

Would you rather...

have a bug fly into
your nose
OR
have a bug fly into
your mouth?

Would you rather…

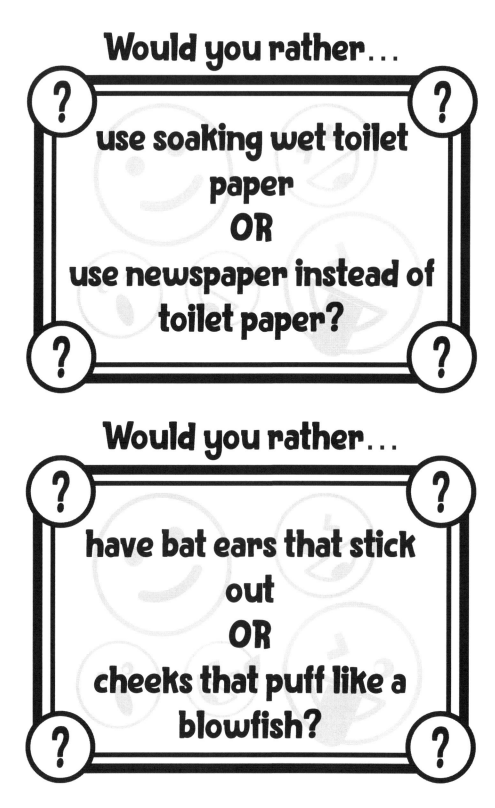

use soaking wet toilet
paper
OR
use newspaper instead of
toilet paper?

Would you rather…

have bat ears that stick
out
OR
cheeks that puff like a
blowfish?

Would you rather...

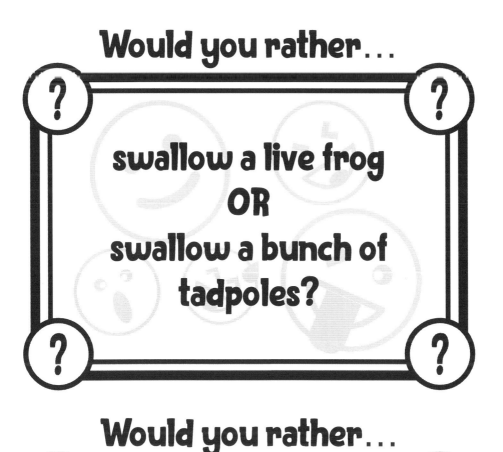

swallow a live frog
OR
swallow a bunch of tadpoles?

Would you rather...

have skin that sheds like a snake
OR
have skin that is bumpy like an armadillo?

Would you rather...

have a bucket stuck on
your head for a week
OR
have a bucket stuck on
your bottom for a week?

Would you rather...

drop your phone in a
toilet
OR
drop your phone in a pile
of dog poo?

Would you rather...

always press elevator
buttons with your tongue
OR
flush every toilet with
your tongue?

Would you rather...

have an extra mouth on
your chest
OR
an extra nose on your
forehead?

Would you rather...

eat a frozen hot dog
OR
drink hot ice cream?

Would you rather...

always have peanut
butter stuck in your
mouth
OR
always have corn stuck
between your teeth?

Printed in Great Britain
by Amazon